TABLE OF CONTENTS

Top 20 Test Taking Tips

1. Carefully follow all the test registration procedures
2. Know the test directions, duration, topics, question types, how many questions
3. Setup a flexible study schedule at least 3-4 weeks before test day
4. Study during the time of day you are most alert, relaxed, and stress free
5. Maximize your learning style; visual learner use visual study aids, auditory learner use auditory study aids
6. Focus on your weakest knowledge base
7. Find a study partner to review with and help clarify questions
8. Practice, practice, practice
9. Get a good night's sleep; don't try to cram the night before the test
10. Eat a well balanced meal
11. Know the exact physical location of the testing site; drive the route to the site prior to test day
12. Bring a set of ear plugs; the testing center could be noisy
13. Wear comfortable, loose fitting, layered clothing to the testing center; prepare for it to be either cold or hot during the test
14. Bring at least 2 current forms of ID to the testing center
15. Arrive to the test early; be prepared to wait and be patient
16. Eliminate the obviously wrong answer choices, then guess the first remaining choice
17. Pace yourself; don't rush, but keep working and move on if you get stuck
18. Maintain a positive attitude even if the test is going poorly
19. Keep your first answer unless you are positive it is wrong
20. Check your work, don't make a careless mistake

Administration of Client Legal Matters

Conflict of interest

A conflict of interest exists when you hold information that may be harmful to your client if it got into the wrong hands. If, for instance, you are familiar with a case or a client while working for one firm, and then change firms and represent the other side, you have a conflict of interest. This can also be the case if you are somehow related to a client, opponent, or someone representing them.

It is your responsibility to keep track of the cases you work on, and review them with new employers if you change jobs. It is also your responsibility to notify your employer as soon as you are aware of a conflict of interest so that the employer, client, or court if necessary, can determine whether or not you may proceed to work on the case. It is your responsibility to be aware of the rules set by the American Bar Association regarding conflicts of interest, so that you are able to identify them and take necessary action.

Client file organization

The way a client file is to be organized greatly depends on the firm, the type of client, and the individual lawyer. For instance, some cases require research, exhibits, and information provided by the client, while others may depend on medical records and police reports. You must find a way to keep these different pieces of information separate and easily attainable, and develop a way to be consistent.

You may choose to tab files chronologically, or you may choose to develop separate files altogether for different time periods depending on the case. You may also keep separate files for each witness or report. The most important point in your choice of organizational strategy is that you are able to locate and provide information quickly as it is needed. Original documents should be maintained as they are, and recent documents must be at your fingertips.

Docket control systems

An attorney's office relies heavily on the docket control system to track dates for court appearances and trials, as well as other important deadlines. A good docket control system will be updated regularly, and include reminders and follow ups so that no appointment or appearance is overlooked. This is important in maintaining client satisfaction, and avoiding malpractice.

Many firms maintain a computerized docket control system, and it is also suggested that attorneys keep regular print outs so that they are aware of tight deadlines in case of computer failure.

Calendars

The three types of calendars normally used are:
- Master: A master calendar typically follows the schedules of all attorneys in a law office so that they can be located and so that they are not double booked. The date, time, and location, and case identification, as well as contact information for the appropriate attorney are all helpful on this master calendar.
- Primary: This calendar shows the appointments on the master calendar as they apply to an individual attorney.
- Secondary: This calendar shows personal appointments and reminders as they apply to an individual attorney. This may be included on the primary calendar depending on preference.
-

Tickler systems

The best way to keep all of these appointments in order and unmissed is to maintain a "tickler system," or reminder system appropriate for each type of appointment and individual the appointment is for.

It is also important that reminders go to more than one attorney so that if one is out, a deadline is still met. As with the rest of the docket control, a tickler system may be maintained manually, or by computer. Both choices require daily maintenance and review of all calendars, and distribution of necessary reminders. It is also your responsibility to know local court rulings on deadlines when they fall on holidays or weekends, as they may vary. The best way to ensure that all tasks are completed is to leave them in the tickler system until it is so.

Client databases

A client database holds information in an organized form that can be easily manipulated to run reports and retrieve client information. It may be used to review many records at once, or to group fields within the records for things such as mailing labels and forms.

A summary database holds small amounts of information on many items, and can easily run on a normal computer. Typically, a summary database is all that is necessary for maintaining client information. A full-text database holds entire documents, and requires a more mature operating system. The appropriate database for you may be determined by your individual needs, and by cost. You must then determine the fields needed in each record, and input appropriate information as it is available. Be sure to keep the client information included confidential.

Event coordination

It is your responsibility to keep the calendar and to keep lists straight, and to use them in a way that allows you to manage workflow efficiently. For instance, you want to create a to-do list that allows you to see deadlines and helps you to prioritize tasks so that those deadlines are met. As you are keeping track of these things for each case, and each attorney, you will have to constantly update your calendar so that you are able to determine what is necessary each day.

You will be working around changing timelines, and depending on deadlines being effectively met by other people as well. You will also need to keep track of contacts so that as things change, you are able to coordinate new plans with appropriate people. The best way for a paralegal to maintain effective time management is with an organized to do list. You must be constantly aware of the goings on in the law office, and able to change plans, priorities, and deadlines accordingly.

A good paralegal will be well read on individual cases, and aware of what is appropriate for him or her to discuss with the attorney. It is important that a paralegal investigates the answers to questions they may have, and describes concerns is clear, correct English. Know the sources you have at hand, such as agencies and courts you deal with on a regular basis. If you are in charge of coordinating events in a case, you must be aware of the laws that help create deadlines, and the network of sources around you such as other attorneys, databases, and even the library. It is also important that you maintain client confidentiality when using your network of resources to coordinate events of a case.

Development of Client Legal Matters

Interviews

Through conducting a potential client interview, you will help the lawyer determine whether or not it is appropriate to represent that client. It is very important that you listen to the potential client to separate fact from fiction, feelings from actuality and, most importantly, to gain the trust of that potential client. That client has likely been through something traumatic, and needs to know that you are listening to what he or she is saying with the intention to help. Assure the client that what he or she shares is confidential and help make him or her comfortable by speaking on the same level.

You must come into the interview with as much knowledge of the type of case and facts within that case as you can. Read any information already collected in the file, and research the appropriate field of interest if necessary. Determine with the attorney who will be conducting the interview, and set up a sight that is conducive to appropriating authority and making the client feel comfortable. Choose a site that encourages the client to understand the confidentiality that exists, and make him or her feel important by putting other tasks aside during the interview.

Determine what you need to know from the client, and make notes before, during, and after the interview accordingly. If the client needs to provide documentation of events or transactions, be sure to communicate that to him or her prior to meeting.

Do all that you can to make the client feel comfortable with sharing information. Be sure to maintain the importance of confidentiality. Stay on the client's level and ask easy questions at the beginning. Phrase questions so that the client must explain situations in detail, but do not assume anything. Leave questions open ended, and pay close attention not only to what your client tells you, but also how he or she is saying it. Keep it simple, for your own sake, and for that of the client. Clarify answers by repeating in your own words to avoid misunderstandings, and to be sure you are taking down valid information.

Investigation resources

The client is your first source of information. Be sure to get as much information from your client as possible, and maintain open communication. Close relatives and friends of your client may also prove to be good sources as an extension of your client himself. Also check with doctors, co-workers, or other people who may be familiar with your client, depending on the type of case you are investigating. You may also research your local library, the internet, as well as past case files at your own firm. Be sure to document findings as you come across them, and keep them organized so that they can be pieced together later. You will want to write up an analysis of your findings for the benefit of the attorney and client.

Legal and factual analysis

Legal analysis requires you to evaluate the client's situation, and find a law that will allow you to take the course of action best suited for the case. You must apply the law exactly as it is stated. This requires a good working knowledge of the law, as well as investigation of past cases with similar characteristics. Factual analysis includes documenting the course of events that apply to your case as you know them, in order. It also may include citing a cast of characters with pertinent information about their relationships to the client and the case, as well as contact information, etc. You will also need to identify a cause of action to be sure that the case can be built on legal grounds.

Client-paralegal relationships

The paralegal should be available to the client for questions and concerns, serving as a middle man between client and attorney. You must give information that you compile in your research to the client so that he or she is aware of how the case is being built, but must be careful not to give legal advice unless it is coming from the attorney. You will be sharing your research with the attorney, and able to relay information about legal options to the client. Throughout your open communication with the client, you should keep organized notes of conversations that may need to be relayed to the attorney, or may help in building your research for the case.

Expert witnesses

An expert witness is a person who, through education or experience, has acquired more than average information on a topic with which your case is concerned. You will work with the attorney to determine what information is needed from the expert, and work with the expert to provide him or her with other research you have obtained regarding the case. Be sure to give the expert valid information so that he or she can develop an informed opinion on the matter. This in mind, be sure to still maintain confidentiality and respect the attorney-client privilege when necessary.

Contract law

A contract is an agreement between two parties that is holds up in court. It may be up for interpretation based on the circumstances in which it was agreed upon and how it is written, though it may also be oral. It is important to note that a written contract cannot be legally changed through an oral transaction. This can be clarified using The Uniform Commercial Code, or UCC. A valid contract must include an offer by one party to provide something for another.

The second party must then accept the offer or negotiate until there is agreement. Then each party must provide compensation for the receipt of their side of the agreement.

Tort law

A tort is a wrong doing by one member of society that causes harm to another member of society either physically, emotionally, or mentally. The most common tort is negligence. The court may decide to settle such a case by awarding compensation, or damages, to the offended party. This is based on recognition that the offending party was aware of the danger and neglected to protect others. The court will determine the severity of negligence, and damages will then reflect the findings. Most extreme damages are awarded if the negligence was with carried out with intent to harm, and least extreme damages are awarded if the offended party was acting without concern for his or her own safety in the first place.

Estate law

Estate law is based on probate, or the validity of a will, and respective distribution of the personal property of a deceased client. Probate laws exist to prove validity of existing wills, and also to provide a guideline for distributing a person's assets if he or she dies without a valid will, or intestate. It is up to the executor of the will to follow through with the requests of the deceased. When a will is created, a person may choose to set up trusts in the names of beneficiaries in order to avoid some taxes. In this case, the trust funds would be transferred to the beneficiaries as the executor distributes all portions of the estate.

Corporations

In a corporation the owners are able to completely separate their personal finances from that of the business. This sets it apart from other ways of owning a business. It is comprised of shareholders, who may see profits and losses as the business does, but cannot be held accountable personally if the business fails. The corporation must file articles of incorporation explaining its intentions as a business, as well as its owners. This must be kept up to date with the government. The corporation is not necessarily run by the owners or shareholders, but by a board of appointed directors.

Case management

As a paralegal, it is your responsibility to keep all information pertaining to a case organized and in tact. You must create a filing system which allows you to easily retrieve documents as they are needed. This file must also provide an organized way for the attorney to view pertinent information to the case. It is important that you model your case management system after that of the firm you are working for. This allows the attorney to be familiar with files from one to the next. Forms to help you keep organized can be found in your local library, and will allow you to create a standard. You may track all of this on paper, or by computer, depending on your firm. Computerized filing systems allow much faster retrieval, and all original documents to be maintained and protected.

Collecting documents

The paralegal will often have to do additional research to fill in missing information in a file. It is very important that you document your work as you retrieve information. If you need to request information from your client or another source, do so in writing. Be sure that your request gets to the hands of someone who can satisfy it, and that he or she is a reliable source. Make note of the source, and the date you receive each document in a running log. Be sure that documents handed over to you are maintained, and that you have any necessary explanations attached to the original document. You will need to thoroughly review each document to determine if it is complete, or if you need further research or explanation. You will also need to mark documents if they are privileged to be sure that others reviewing the file will know this as well.

Providing documents

When the opposing client makes a request for documents, it is the paralegal's duty to provide them. In most cases, you will have 30 days to do so, though the court may allow longer, or require faster turn around. Depending on the length and complexity of the documents requested, you may choose to copy them yourself, or to hire out the job. Either way, it should be done at the expense of the opposing party, and not that of your client. Be sure to keep track of which documents you have provided to the opposing party by making note in the client file. Also be sure not to provide information that is confidential to your client or to the firm. If such a document is requested, you can contest the request through the court, and will normally find you are protected from providing that information. In some cases, you may redact only a portion of the document, and provide the remainder for the opposing party to see. Be sure to keep track of what is redacting for your own reference as well.

Legal document types

Exhibits: Exhibits must be organized in a way that the attorney needs them, and in a way that you can easily locate them, to be used as evidence during a trial. They must be marked according to the specific court's requirements. Affidavits or Declarations: Though both types of statements require that the person quoted promises truth, an affidavit is also made before a court officer.

You must also declare that you believe the information to be true as it is presented.

Contracts: This is an agreement enforceable by law. If you are creating a contract, be sure to be consistent, clear, and leave no room for different interpretations, so that both parties are under the same understanding.

Articles of Incorporation: The format varies from one state to the next. Check the laws that pertain to your state. You also must include the name of the corporation and the incorporator, the intentions of the corporation, and the estimated value.

Deeds: This states ownership of land. Include a property description, and any other requirements in your state.

Forecasts: This is generally a budget projection requested by a corporation. This must be approved by an attorney before being presented to the client.

Documents deadlines

Depending on the type of document, and the specific court, rules on how to file and serve documents, as well as when to do so will vary. There are some general rules that will apply to your calculations. First, the date of an event or document request is not included in a measurement of time. The time starts the day following the event. Second, the last day (for instance, day 30 of a 30 day deadline) is included in your calculation, unless it is a day when court is closed. Third, if the time frame provided is 0-10 days, the days court is closed in that count are not included. Fourth, identify legal holidays appropriately, including days that are government appointed. Fifth, if you receive a request by mail, add 3 days to the deadline.

Filing complaints

The purpose of the complaint is to notify the defendant of the claim against him. This should be a concise statement explaining the grounds for complaint, and request for judgment. It must include the name of the person/corporation filing the complaint, as well as the person/corporation in the defense. A complaint may also request that a case is heard by a federal court, provided that the case meets necessary requirements. The complaint must be filed in a state where the parties reside, or where the incident causing complaint took place. Once a complaint is filed with the court, the court commences with the case, and documents will be served to the defendant.

Servicing complaints

A complaint may be serviced by any legal adult not associated with the case. The attorney may also request that it is serviced by an officer of the United States. The complaint and summons must be serviced to the defendant within 120 days of filing. The service is usually done by physically handing the defendant the complaint, or leaving it at their place of residence. In the case of a corporation, complaints would be serviced to the appropriate officer. It may also be left with the defending attorney, or clerk at the office of that attorney. Once the complaint is serviced, a certificate of service is furnished for documentation.

Responding to complaints

Response is required within 20 days after service, with exception if the 20th day falls on a weekend or court holiday. You may choose to motion to dismiss the case, or to request further information before providing a response. If you choose to provide an answer, the purpose will be to deny the claims brought against the defendant. Each allegation must be denied, or it is considered admitted. If a defendant wants to make only a partial denial or admittance, that can also be done. The defendant can choose to make an affirmative defense in order to protect him or herself if the complaint is true.

Discovery plans

The parties will consult with one another to devise a discovery plan. They may agree to provide information at this point in partial disclosure. This allows them to avoid waiting for a discovery request that would come with a deadline. They must provide the opposing party with contact information for individuals involved in the case, and a description of documents they have in possession and are using to build their case. They must also provide the opposing party with contact information for each witness, including experts, and exhibits which will be used in trial. Following the pre-trial conference, you will generally have 14 days to furnish these documents.

Discovery

There are different types of discoveries. These types include:

- Interrogatories: These are formally written questions by the opposing party, and must be formally answered under oath. There is a limit of 25 interrogatories, and they must be answered within 30 days.
- Requests for Productions: One party may request the opportunity to inspect documents, and the opposing party must allow this to happen within 30 days. They do not have to provide copies of documents, but just permission to inspect.
- Requests for Admissions: One party may request that the other party admit to truth of different matters to verify their case.
- Depositions on Written Questions: One party may interview a witness under oath and in writing for the purpose of verifying an argument.
- Depositions: Each party may take 10 oral depositions under oath before the trial. Each must be limited to one day, and in less than 7 hours. If there are documents requested in conjunction with a deposition, the opposing party must furnish those documents by the time the

deposition takes place. A deposition is normally done face to face and is recorded.

Witness preparation

Be sure to provide the witness with information about the trial including directions, time and place, how to dress, etc. You will need to conduct a meeting with the witness to go over the case prior to his or her court appearance. If a witness is not willfully testifying, order court subpoenas. Help the witness feel comfortable with the case, and with what to expect as general court proceedings take place. Make sure to understand and accommodate and specific needs your witness may have. Be careful to share only necessary information with your witness, as the communications are not protected. Review the case and documents that pertain to each witness's testimony. Go over questions and answers that will come up while on trial. You should practice running through possible questions to put your witness at ease the day of the trial.

Preparing witness files

You will want to prepare an individual file for each witness in advance of your meetings with them. In this file include any information you have about the witness, and what information he or she has as it relates to the case. Attorneys will vary in what information they require in the witness file, but what is important is that you are able to easily locate information about a witness to help the attorney prepare for meeting the witness. If an attorney plans to use specific evidence along with a given witness, that evidence should be identified in the witness file as well. Also make note of any possible cross-examinations you foresee, and draft possible questions. The purpose of preparing a witness file is to help prepare the attorney for the witness preparation meeting.

Preparing for real estate closing

Be sure to make yourself aware of particular laws in your state with regard to real estate transactions. Parties present at the closing will include buyer, seller, and their respective attorneys. You will need to include documents that show intent to sell, intent to purchase, and any financing information in a file prepared for the closing meeting. You may also want to summarize the goals of the closing meeting in the form of a check list for the attorney so that he or she can go through each step individually with the buyers and sellers.

Legal proceedings role

The paralegal's role in legal proceedings will vary some depending on the attorney. Most of the time, your role begins with great organization. You will want to be sure that all deadlines are met, and all files are readily available before the proceeding begins, so that the attorney is not caught off guard. You may also help the attorney be keeping the client comfortable during the proceeding. You may answer questions the client has, or pass them along to the attorney at the appropriate times. You will also be responsible for keeping the entire legal team in check with one another. You may choose to give them a written report at the beginning of each day so they are aware of what to expect. You may also take notes during proceedings on all that is going on in the court room from testimonies and demonstrative evidence presented, to jurors' responses.

Early resolution

It is in the best interest of the client to settle matters as soon as possible, and out of court. Most courts require that both parties attempt to settle the dispute through mediation or other means at some point before going to trial. There are professional mediators who will help in this matter. You may choose to meet with the attorney and opposing party prior to seeking professional mediation, in order to hear the full argument and interests of the other side, and determine if you may reach an agreement independently. Otherwise, forms of alternative dispute resolution include settlement conferences, mediation through a third party, arbitration where each side can present their case to an arbitrator and hear a decision, mini-trials similar to arbitration, and summary jury trials where each party can present its case to a jury and hear a decision. These are all ways in which you can hear the arguments of each side in hopes of reaching an agreement that works out of court. The sooner this is done, the less damage there is to your client both financially and emotionally.

Using past legal authorities

Finding a similar case heard in another court previously can help argue your case if the findings match what you are looking for. You will want to find a case that has similar claims. It is also important to find a case that was heard in a respectable court by a respectable judge if possible. You will want to analyze key elements of the case, and make note of similarities and differences to your own. Then you can base your argument on the findings in that case by highlighting the parallels for the jury. Hearing that another jury found a defendant, in a similar situation to yours "not guilty," is a powerful way to persuade your own jury to see things the same way.

Citing authorities

Proper citations of legislative documents may vary from state to state. For the most part, they follow the same format as that of citing the United States Constitution. Proper citation guidelines can be found in the Bluebook. Judicial opinions must include the case name, volume, reporter, page and date. Citations for restatements, opinions, and uniform laws all follow similar guidelines, and must include the name of the law or volume in which it was found, page number, and date. You may choose to use short form citations throughout your research if you are citing the same source repeatedly. It only needs to be formally cited the first time. As a paralegal, you will find it necessary to verify the format of citations in research for your attorney.

Client Matters- important terms

Attorney-Client Privilege: This is a privilege of the client, so that he or she may understand that anything disclosed to the attorney or paralegal will be kept in confidence unless it is discussed openly. This allows the client to give the attorney information to create a case, while using discretion as to what information needs to be public. This privilege extends beyond the time frame in which the case is handled.

Physician-Patient Privilege: This is a privilege of a patient, so that he or she may choose not to share information discussed with a doctor.

Attorney Work Product: This is a privilege of the attorney, so that he or she is not obligated to share select information found regarding a law suit.

Authorizations and Releases: It may be necessary for you to obtain these during your initial client interview. Normally these forms are used to get permission from a client to obtain medical documents, or other such documents that may otherwise be confidential.

Court Decisions reflect the decision made by a judge regarding a specific set of facts.

Statutes are based on prior cases, but can be applied to many circumstances and are up for interpretation as they are applied to future cases.

Jurisdiction determines whether or not a particular court can hear a case.

Venue is simply the actual place where the trial will take place.

Literal interpretation refers to application of a law based upon the exact words as it is written.

Intrinsic factors are those points that may not be found in the literal interpretation of the law, but in the way the court came to the decision it did.

Standing refers to whether or not one person has a right to sue another.

Legal capacity states that that person must also be emotionally and physically healthy and aware of the case at hand.

Sole Proprietorship: This type of organization can have only one owner, and that owner's personal finances are shared with the business. When the business makes money, the owner makes money. If the business has debts, they are shared by the owner as well.

Partnership: In a general partnership, both parties own equal parts in the business, and have the same liabilities as with a sole proprietor, only they are shared among more than one owner. A limiter partnership is similar, only there is one partner who carries a larger burden of liability, while the other sees profits and losses based on investment into the business.

Limited Liability Company: As with the limited partnership, liability reflects investment. However, each member of the business may share equal investment if they so choose.

Subpoena: This is a written request ordered through the court that a particular person shows up as a witness in court. They are generally used to require witnesses to appear in court who would otherwise deny a request made by an attorney alone. Only subpoena witnesses who are competent to testify.

Evidence: Any piece of documentation or matter which makes an argument more viable.

Hearsay: A statement made out of court that is not admissible as evidence.

Allegation: A claim that must be proven during trial.

Jury Selection: Attorneys or judges will interview potential jurors to determine who will hear a particular trial.

Opening Statement: Presented by the attorney at the start of a trial, this statement outlines the claims that the party plans to prove throughout the proceeding.

Burden of Proof: This refers to the idea that the prosecution's job on trial is to prove its allegations against the defendant, who is innocent until they prove otherwise.

Closing Statement: A summary of argument presented by the attorney at the close of the trial

Bench Trial: A trial by judge with no jury.

Impeachment: A claim that a witness is not fit or truthful in testimony.

Leading Questions: A question worded in a way that it encourages a particular response.

Judicial Notice: The court recognizes some facts to be true, and therefore does not require evidence pertaining to them.

Factual and Legal Research

Obtaining facts

The attorney will fill you in on the relevant facts as he or she knows them, and it is your job then to build on those facts, verify them, and find more information. You may do so by interviewing your client and others involved in the case. You will want to use these interviews to determine what further research may need to be conducted as you learn the "who, what, when, and where" of the case. You will want to keep a current document noting your findings, and separating your facts by determining which are relevant to the case. You will also need to determine how the relevant facts relate to the law based on what your client is claiming to have happened, and what type of compensation he or she is seeking.

Analysis of facts

You should keep an organized notebook of research as it is conducted, and determine what evidence can be and needs to be obtained. That evidence, such as contracts, communication between parties, and any physical evidence or should be summarized as it pertains to the case. It is your job to analyze the facts and determine what is relevant. You must then include only the relevant information in your final statement describing the facts of the case. Relevant information may include descriptions of the parties involved as they were prior to the claims as well. You will have to continually edit your analysis of facts as you complete your research and determine relevance accordingly.

Legal authorities

The types of legal authorities include:
- Primary authorities include written law.

- Secondary authorities include other reliable sources for research.
- Attorney's general opinions are written on topics that are for consideration in each state and may or may not pertain to your case.
- Dictionaries and thesauri may help you define terms and better explain your case.
- A legal dictionary may even point you in the direction of previous cases that could be helpful.
- Directories published by the American Bar Association will help you locate experts in your field of interest.
- Legal encyclopedias will give you a description of different legal concerns and how they are applied in your local court.
- Periodicals may give you some insight into past cases and outcomes.
- Restatements will provide you with detailed explanation of previous court decisions.
- Treatises will zero in on one particular legal topic and explain it in great detail.

Primary authorities

Primary authorities include both mandatory and persuasive authorities. Mandatory authority includes laws that must be followed by citizens of your state. If a law is broken, this is argument for you case. Persuasive authority includes laws that you may find in other states, to use as argument even if they are not present in your own state. These are not laws that citizens of your state are required to follow, however they may help your attorney argue the case if they are relevant and clear. If an attorney uses such a law in an attempt to persuade a judge, the court may decide to apply the law of another state if it reflects the general beliefs of the particular court.

Sources of authorities

Law in the United States can be found in a number of sources.

- In addition to the United States Constitution, each state has a constitution as well.
- Past legislation and statutes can be found on the city, state, and national levels.
- Administrative authority includes agency regulations on the city, state, and federal levels as well.
- Executive orders are those followed by administrative agencies as issued by the President.
- Treaties include an agreement between the United States and a foreign country.
- Court rules of procedure are found on both a state and national level, and are determined by the supreme courts. They must be followed as present.

Judicial Authority

A law is determined by a court based on past circumstances and decisions. It must then be written and published as law. Many laws are applied as written, and citizens are expected to follow them. In a case where the law is not followed and a person is brought to trial because of it, the court is then in a position to interpret the law as it applies to the particular case, and make a decision based on that interpretation. This interpretation may be applied as a statute in a subsequent case. Thus it is somewhat up to the court to develop an opinion on each case individually. If the court makes a decision based on previous hearings of similar cases, those cases are called precedent. By establishing precedents, amending laws with statutes, and interpreting laws as they are written, it is the responsibility of the court to remain consistent from one case to the next. You will want to identify such information in your research so that it can be readily presented to the court as part of your argument in your client's defense.

Court opinion structure

The structure of published court opinions is standard. It will include the name of the case, the date the court reached a decision, the docket number as assigned by the particular court, a short summary of the case, a short summary of the legal arguments in the case, names of the attorneys involved in the case, names of the judges who heard the case, and the final opinion of the court. The opinion of the court will often include the relevant facts presented in the case, the ways in which the law applies to those facts, and the opinion of the court based on analysis of those facts. The court will often provide an opinion on each individual issue involved in the case before stating an overall decision or opinion.

Published cases

You may find cases published in a variety of sources such as digests and legal encyclopedias. A digest will organize cases by the legal issue at hand. They have extensive indexes which allow you to search key terms in your case, and locate past cases involving the same concepts. You would want to begin by searching digests in your own state, but may also find digests outlining cases heard in other states helpful. This is true particularly if there are not many similar cases in your own state. American Law Reports also publishes cases and gives extensive opinion and research regarding the legal issues of each case.

Legal analysis role

You must familiarize yourself with relevant statutes and laws in your state as they pertain to your case. You must then identify other cases that may be relevant, and apply them to your argument. Some cases may be more relevant, or deemed more valuable than others depending on factors such as the judge and the court where the case was heard, and how opinions on similar cases may have evolved over time. For proper legal analysis, you must complete the four steps of the IRAC process. Those four steps are: identifying the issues and rules that apply to your case, analyzing them, and developing a conclusion.

Factual and Legal Writing

Communication

It is your responsibility to listen well and convey information clearly in order to carry out your job effectively. You must be sure that when you are explaining facts to your attorney, or requesting information in a client interview, that you are clear and confident. It is important not only to state your needs clearly, but also to convey confidence through body language and inflection. This will create an atmosphere in which you will get the most reliable information, with the most ease. It is also very important that you pay attention to body language and inflection when you are listening to an attorney or client. You should keep yourself focused and give the speaker your undivided attention.

Telephone communication

You will use the telephone frequently to communicate with your client. You will need to be diligent about returning calls, and making yourself available over the phone so that you can obtain facts about the case as they are available, and answer any questions or relay information that your client may have for your attorney. It is important to display proper manners, and be respectful of other people's time. You should be well organized before making a telephone call if you hope to obtain information from a client. Try not to put callers on hold, but rather hear the information they are looking for, take notes while they are talking, and call them back when you have gathered it. If you must leave a message, do so effectively by giving as much information as possible about your case, and yourself. Spell out words that may not be familiar such as names, and speak clearly when leaving a call back number.

Dictation

Avoid a stream of consciousness approach to your dictations. Rather, you should organize the information you will be dictating beforehand so that you can be concise. Try to minimize background noise, and focus on the dictation. Be mindful of the transcriber who will be hearing your tape, and spell out words or give explanations when necessary. If you would like the transcriber to include grammatical inflection such as italics, or to start a new paragraph in a specific part of a dictation, be sure to explain that as it happens. If you would like articles listed a specific way, you may want to also include a written example for the transcriber.

Paralegal Roles

It is the paralegal's responsibility to be clear in communications with the attorney, and to work hard to meet attorneys' requests. This requires you as the paralegal to take responsibility for understanding what the attorney may be asking for, and that you clarify through clear speech delivery, and active listening. Good communication between the paralegal and attorney will create a much smoother work environment for both. You will be better off taking the time to clarify needs as they are initially being communicated, than to wait and fall under the level of expectations simply because of a misunderstanding. If and when you do make a mistake, try to learn from it, and communicate how you may be able to avoid it in the future.

Workload considerations

Be sure to understand tasks that are assigned before you begin them. If you do not understand what is expected, clarify with the attorney. The guidance you will get through this clarification will save you from spending time worrying over the semantics of instructions, and will get you to the correct starting point fast.

In addition to ensuring that you are able to complete individual assignments efficiently, you also need to be able to manage the volume of assignments you are expected to complete. If you are overcommitted, no assignment will be completed to the best of your ability. If you are asked to do something while in the middle of an ongoing case, it is wise to let the requesting attorney know what you are already responsible for. He may then choose to negotiate deadlines with the attorney you are currently working for, so that you are able to complete both tasks effectively. Be sure to speak up rather than taking on an unrealistic load.

In the event that a paralegal has too much work to complete, the most important thing to do is create a to-do list, and prioritize. This way the most important tasks are completed first, and the workload is managed in an organized manner. There are databases available to help track such a workload, which will in turn help a paralegal to be more efficient, and also to determine when he or she has to turn down a job altogether. An attorney may decide to altar his own deadlines in order to work with a particular paralegal, or he may go to another to get his goal accomplished. It is important to be honest about it if the workload is too large so that attorneys and clients are not made to suffer.

Supervisory roles

Be generally courteous and appreciative of your secretary when you are communicating tasks. Work with her to trouble-shoot areas where mistakes are made in a positive manner. Put yourself on the same level as your secretary or other supporters to create a team environment, rather than one where you are demanding all the time. Give credit where credit is due. Be considerate of the secretary's work load, just as you expect attorneys to be considerate of your own. If the secretary is working on something for another supervisor, understand that yours will have to come next. It is best to keep an open line of communication with the secretary so that work is done the way you expect it to be done.

Communication with client

Though the attorney often is the one who holds the legal answers to a client's needs, the paralegal is able to handle most of the day to day communications. This allows a client to feel his or her needs are being met by someone familiar with the case and allow the attorney to maintain a busy schedule not always conducive to returning client phone calls each day.

Keep record of all correspondence with the client, be it print or vocal communication. If the client is seeking legal advice, it is beyond your realm of expertise. You will act as a liaison between the client and attorney in this case. Though this requires you to obtain information from the attorney for the client, you are now in control of the turn around time. You can convey the question in a way that will elicit a direct response, minimizing the time it takes for the attorney to respond, and for the client to wait.

Language usage

The paralegal must be well spoken, using proper English at all times. You must communicate clearly and concisely to avoid misunderstanding, and to convey that you are intelligent and competent. Pay close attention to written detail, and use correct grammar just as you might check your spelling. Also, avoid using legal terms that often act as fillers without adding any information to a sentence. They are not only unimpressive, but create confusion for most readers. When you need to convey specific details, you do not want to bore your reader.

Though pronouns are okay to use, be sure to be clear about who or what they refer to. For instance, if you are talking about more than one man in an altercation, refer to them by name, rather than "he" to avoid confusion. It is better to take the time to effectively communicate a point the first time around, than to create ambiguity, and lose your audience's attention. Be sure that nouns and verbs match within your sentence structure as well. If a verb refers to a plural noun, the verb must be plural as well. Be sure to link verbs to the correct subject of the sentence to ensure that this is done properly.

To be the most effective, keep things simple enough that any reader can understand. Write about things formally, but keep in mind how you might talk about them as well and avoid writing in a way that would not make sense in plain speech. If you must use legal jargon, you must also explain what it means for the unfamiliar reader. Even a highly educated reader may not understand such jargon if he or she is not in a profession that deals with law. Be sure to use correct grammar and proofread your writing. Finally, if you are responding to a letter that may be less than kind, maintain your high level of professionalism, and reply in a neutral way that will represent you and your attorney effectively and respectfully.

While keeping everything well-documented is a good thing in most cases, you must also be aware that anyone may read your correspondence in time. Choose language carefully and avoid insulting others. Be very careful not to give legal advice in a letter signed by you, as it is only appropriate if it comes from the attorney. Also keep in mind that you are the paralegal, not the attorney. Do not make promises you do not have the authority to make or cannot carry through. If you write them, you have to take responsibility for them. Only give information necessary to make your point. Do not use extra verbiage, and do not give extra information.

Grammar Considerations

Negatives: A negative in a sentence explains what is not done. Be sure to avoid using two negatives in a sentence, or a double negative, as that correctly translates to a positive. Not only is this grammatically incorrect, but it is also difficult for your reader to understand what you actually mean.

Nominalization: This is the unnecessary use of a verb to convey a noun. It uses more words than necessary to convey a point. Use as few words as possible.

Parallel Construction: This allows you to convey multiple ideas using the same sentence structure. You may begin your sentence, and then list multiple ideas that could all be added to the same preceding words. Be sure that each parallel idea is written in a way that, if stated individually, would be grammatically correct.

Infinitives: The infinitive form of a verb includes "to." For instance, "to go" is the infinitive of the verb "go." Be sure not to split up the two parts of an infinitive within a sentence. This ensures clarity of the verb.

Case: This reflects whether the noun is the subject or object of a sentence.

Possessive Pronouns: You may show possession through a word such as "his," or through adding an apostrophe, or an apostrophe followed by "s" to the end of the word possessing the noun.

That and Which: A clause that uses "that" is restrictive in what it refers to, whereas "which" is more general.

Modifiers: Modifiers are words which further clarify an expression. They should be placed in front of the phrase they are clarifying.

Participles: A participle is a phrase that describes modifies a clause. They should be placed with the phrase they are modifying.

It is important to be mindful of your use of all three of these concepts. Otherwise, your sentences can convey an entirely different idea than you intended.

Compound Phrases: These are multiple words used together to convey one idea. Often hyphens help clarify which words belong together in a sentence.

Conjunctions: Such as "both" and "and," when used in conjunction with each other, be sure to use the same structure. For instance, each should be followed by a verb, or each should be followed by a noun.

Run-On Sentences: Avoid run-on sentences by separating individual ideas into individual sentences. Keep it simple. If you want to include more than one idea in a sentence, use the word "and" to separate them.

Dangling Prepositions: If you can avoid ending a sentence with a preposition, do so. More importantly, pay attention to how the sentence reads. If it conveys your point accurately and flows well, it is probably fine.

Comma: This can be used to separate ideas in a list, or to separate concepts in a sentence. A comma usually falls where you might pause as you read.

Semicolon: This signifies a pause or separation greater than that expressed with a comma. You may use it instead of a period in order to link two points in one sentence.

Colon: Generally, a colon introduces a list or subject to follow it.

Dashes and Hyphens: These can be used to connect two parts of a word, or two phrases in a sentence. Following one phrase, it may indicate that the next phrase is a sentence fragment describing the former.

Quotation Marks: These are used to indicate a quotation, or something spoken by another.

Apostrophes: This may be used to indicate possession, to create a contraction of two words, or to make a number plural.

Brackets and Parentheses: Brackets are used to indicate where parts of a quotation may not be direct, or where information may be missing.

Parentheses are used to include information in a sentence to clarify details.

Ellipses: Ellipses can be used to indicate information left out of a direct quote. They should never be used at the beginning of a quote, but may be used at the end.

Slash: Used to represent "or."

Capitalization: Be sure to capitalize proper nouns such as the name of a person or place. Certain nouns are always capitalized as well, such as President or God when they are used in short for "President of the United States."

It is very important that throughout your entire work on a given case, you document everything you do in writing. There are formal ways to document many of the tasks you will complete, and you can often find forms that are already created for the same purpose.

You will find many forms at your library, and your own firm may even retain copies of past letters and documents so that they are available to mimic in the future as well. While forms are a great way to ensure proper documentation and correct wording, you must also be sure to keep the information in your new document relevant to your specific case.

No matter how small or seemingly insignificant the conversation may be, any time you talk with someone regarding your case, create a memo to attach to the file. Do it promptly so that you do not forget the conversation, or forget to do it at all. Either type your memos, or write them legibly on a full piece of paper so that they are easily attainable if needed. Having things in writing will help you track events in your case, and also make others who may be looking over the file aware of all information. This allows your attorney to also take responsibility for knowing what is going on with the case.

Letter-writing

When writing letters, you want to avoid using legal jargon that does not add to the point. Letters should be easily understood by the reader. Be sure to use proper grammar and spelling, and proofread any document before sending it off. You want your letter to be a representation of the professionalism you stand for, as it represents both you and the firm. Do not use slang or a stream-of-consciousness style of writing. If you are sending the client copies of information in the file, you must also include a cover letter both for the purpose of describing what you are sending, and to have a copy that can be retained for your file, as record that the document was sent. Be clear and concise if you are asking the client for a response. Number your requests and give specific instruction to avoid confusion.

There are three common mistakes made in letter writing. Being aware of them will help you to avoid them yourself. The first mistake to avoid is under explaining what you are saying to the reader of the letter. Be sure to explain everything well, especially if your reader knows nothing about the case, or nothing about law. Be sure to introduce people you may discuss, and explain concepts that you yourself may find obvious, as they may not be to your reader. The second mistake to avoid is patronizing your reader. Though you want to explain concepts your reader may not be familiar with, you also need to be careful not to over explain things that are obvious. The third mistake to avoid is ambiguity about any requests you are making. Be sure to clearly list requests, and explain where and when things are to be done so that your reader can complete your requests confidently and without delay.

Be sure that all of your correspondence is professional, even if the matter is simple, or the client is a friend. This ensures that you are representing yourself and your attorney in a respectful way, and your clients will trust you more because of it. You want to exude confidence and organization in your writing. Always address clients and attorneys or colleagues formally in writing, not by their first name or nickname. This applies to everyone you correspond with professionally, no matter how close a friend they may be outside of work.

Keep writing as simple as possible. Place verbs next to subjects and avoid using extra adjectives and adverbs. Avoid the temptation to make your writing sound "smart," and instead use common vocabulary that everyone understands. Use short sentences that are easy to follow and make a single point. Do not include any word in a sentence that does not add to the meaning. Be sure to only use words for which you are sure of the meaning. Avoid using words that are commonly used incorrectly unless you are aware of the rules that apply to their use.

Positive techniques, when used correctly, can enhance your writing. Using a word repeatedly in a paragraph can help emphasize that word, and help make a stronger point. After reading a word over and over, the reader associates that word with the overall suggestion of the writing. You may also choose to repeat a word twice in a row in the same sentence to enhance its importance. Repetition can also be used with one letter as in alliteration. This can draw attention to particular words that a reader might otherwise skim over. Choose words carefully so that they evoke the feeling in the reader that you intend.

When writing for the court, choose words that will keep the reader's attention. Swap synonyms for words you might use in every day speaking, for words that are more descriptive. Though you must keep your story truthful, it is your job to write in a way that illustrates what you want to court to understand. The right word can be very persuasive. You can use words to point out details in your story that may seem otherwise unimportant. Avoid using direct quotations whenever possible. It is rare to find a case exactly the same as yours, and you are better off summarizing similarities for your argument and applying them to the case at hand.

Proofreading

Proofreading helps to maintain the high level of professionalism required in this venue. Simple mistakes can be avoided by looking back over work. Not only will proofreading help you to avoid small spelling and grammatical errors, but it will also ensure that you are writing clearly and that a reader can understand your point. If you read back over your writing and it leaves you confused, go back and make it simpler. It is also a good idea to have another person proofread to make sure a neutral reader can follow your writing. Sometimes it is difficult for you to catch problem areas since you do know what you are meaning to say. Take time to read slowly and be patient with yourself. It is worth the trouble.

Applying past laws

If a court makes a decision in one case, it will generally uphold that decision in future cases where the situation is similar. Read past legislation as it is written, and apply the law in the same way. Statutes follow a similar rule. They should be read in a simple manner that can clearly be applied to your case. If you can read a law to mean more than one thing, you must generally look to other decisions made by the court and assume that the intended meaning is consistent with them. Be sure that you are analyzing law as it is meant to be read, and not basing your arguments on another writer's opinions. You may write a case brief to cite relevant facts and explanation of the final decision of the court.

Legal memorandums

A legal memorandum is used as an internal document in a law office to answer a question of how a law may be interpreted. When you are searching for cases to cite in a memorandum, choose the most recent cases you can find, as they can hold the most relevance. Find cases with facts similar to yours and analyze them as much as possible. In a memorandum you wan to be sure to give citations for the cases you are analyzing, and use page numbers to help make points so that the reader can refer to them if necessary. Your analysis should lead you to a memorandum that will help anticipate how the court will hear your case and how it will apply past legal authorities. Follow the format set forth by the law firm or attorney you are working for. Include a statement of facts, legal questions brought forth, the court's decision, a presentation of your analysis, and the anticipated result.

Appropriate analysis of a memorandum should be based on facts, not personal bias or opinion. You must provide facts for the reader, and explain a logical path that leads to the court's decision. You must not expect the reader to accept your explanation without reason. Explain the facts of the case in the past tense, and the actual law in the present tense, since it can still apply. Explain how the court rationalized its decision by highlighting the facts that pertain to it. If the court made statements that did not apply to its decision, they may still be used to persuade a court to hear your case differently. You will want to note these opinions of the court as well. In most cases you will find several previous court decisions similar to what you are seeking. You will want to cite these cases to show the abundance of general agreement. This is called a string cite. Ultimately, your analysis should answer a legal question regarding your case, based on the findings in others.

Designations

By designating names for parties or events in a case, you will cut back on confusion. You may choose to refer to the defendant by name, or by simply calling him the defendant, but be consistent. Introduce the person in the beginning of your writing, designate what you intend to refer to him as, and do so from there on out. If there are multiple people within one side of the case, it may be simpler to refer to them by name, or by a description of their part in the story. For instance, if they are a store owner, you could call them "store owner" rather than by name if you prefer. This is called a functional name. If you are referring to an event or group, you may choose to use the first letters of the term or some other abbreviation. Just as with all other writing, keep this simple, consistent, and easy to follow.

Application of legal authority

Legal authority is found either in case law or statutes. Published opinions of the court are useful in analysis of present cases to determine how a court might hear your case. Not all primary authority is in stone. It, along with secondary authority (popular court opinion) is merely a useful predictor. You can still argue your case the way you see it, and apply laws and findings you feel are appropriate, and the court may come to a different decision. Mandatory authority, however, is a legal authority that will always be followed by the court. If you are conducting analysis to answer a legal question, pay attention to all legal authorities that might apply.

Briefs

A legal brief must be used to explain the case to a judge as you see it, and to persuade him to see it the same way. You must keep it to the facts and find a way to present your client's case favorably. You will want to highlight facts that persuade the court to see your client's side of the case, and only quickly mention those which do not. As with all legal writing, keep it simple and concise so that a judge can easily read the brief, understand your point, and hopefully see things the same way.

State the question, and findings, as well as a persuasive description of how those findings were reached. Do not leave holes to create questions for the reader. It is always recommended that you present a written brief if you have the opportunity so that your argument is easily attainable by the judge even after he has heard your case.

You will include the name of the case, and the date of the final decision. Then explain what each side is claiming and seeking from the case. Explain who the judge was who heard the case, or represented the court's opinion. This can consist of one judge speaking on behalf of all, a group of judges that agree on one decision more than any other, or the court setting forth an opinion without attaching a name. Judges may also choose to dissent or concur to highlight their differences. Making note of these things as they are found in previous cases may help you determine how a decision will probably be made in your own case. Finally, define the issue the court is deciding in the case, and how the final decision was reached. The final decision is called the holding, and is often found at the end of the brief. Most importantly, highlight the facts so that you can understand the case itself, and how to apply it to your own.

Each court will have its own set of rules to describe exactly how a brief should be written out. There may be specifications on paper size, the order that information is presented, appropriate length, and so forth. Turning in a brief late, or failing to follow format protocol can cause detriment to a case. It is the paralegal's responsibility to ensure that this is done properly, meeting the individual standards of each court. There may be a brief bank available at the attorney's office. Past briefs can act as a guide for what is acceptable, and may even provide useful phrasing or act as a template for new briefs.

A trial brief is written to answer a question for the court. Researching and writing a trial brief can not only provide necessary information for the court, but it can also help a paralegal and attorney understand the facts of the question at hand, and develop a clear argument. A trial brief may speak to many issues, or only one. This depends on the court rules, as well as the purpose of the brief itself. Keeping things short and simple will help ensure that a judge is able to read over this important research, and understand the connections it draws between the current case, and past cases and authorities. Be sure to follow formalities required by the individual court.

The statement of the facts includes all of the known facts about a case that a judge may need in order to come to a just decision on a particular matter. Therefore, a brief should only include facts relevant to the particular question the brief addresses. The statement of facts is the opportunity to lay out the basis of the legal analysis to follow. Give weight to facts that will help persuade the judge to see things in the client's favor, and give explanation for facts that may not. Provide arguments based on the facts given, and present them in a way that is persuasive, yet truthful.

The proposition is found within the brief, and simply describes the argument to be explained in the coming sentences. It should state the question and the argument firmly, to indicate to the judge the direction of persuasion. If the brief is covering more than one matter, there may be more than one proposition. The first should be the biggest argument with the most support. A brief should have a proposition, then argument, followed by a subproposition, and further argument. The subpropositions should act as a transition to flow into further support for the argument. The propositions should be direct and unwavering. It should explain how and why the court should favor the client, without a doubt.

The argument is the majority of the brief, and explains why the court should see the client's side. It may be preceded by a short summary of the argument, which can act as a powerful section of the brief if well written. It provides a succinct explanation of the argument, allowing the actual body of the argument to act as a reiteration in greater detail if the court needs it. Some courts require both as part of the trial brief, and some require only the formal argument. The purpose of the argument is to persuade the reader to believe the proposition. Present the argument by citing highest laws or applicable statutes first, followed by an analysis of the case in relation to them.

When finalizing the brief, be sure that all citations are documented correctly, especially when accompanying a quotation. Check for and correct all spelling and grammatical errors. Be sure that the brief follows all specifications of the court; from the way it is bound to the order information is presented. Obtain approval of the second draft from the attorney, and proofread again. Have copies made so that there are enough to satisfy the needs of the court and the attorney's office. File the appropriate copy with the clerk, and document the transaction for the file. Add any dates effective from the time the brief is filed in the calendar.

Trial brief vs. appellate brief

An appellate brief is written following a court's decision, in the instance that a case is then heard by an appellate court. It does not consider the facts of the case, but rather the true interpretation of the laws, and how they should fairly be applied. An appeal is based on an argument that the court did not follow proper procedure when coming to the initial decision. An appellate court still needs to know the facts of the case as background in order to determine how the laws should be applied, and to understand why certain appeals are made. The format of the document should be very similar to that of the trial brief, with the addition of a table of contents. There will also be a section listing the questions presented which states the matters for consideration by the appellate court. The appellate brief must also include a section summarizing information about the previous trial and court's decision.

Office Administration

Budgeting

A paralegal must be able to understand projections and budgeting in order to keep clients informed. In most cases, only a general understanding of accounting software and regular budgeting practices for a particular firm is necessary. There is likely an office manual available to the paralegal for study of general accounting practices. This will give such specific information, such as who is responsible for each part of the job. There may be one clerk in charge of billing, another in charge of payroll, and an accountant who oversees all financial matters of the firm. While a general knowledge is helpful, a paralegal still cannot determine exact fees for a client, just as he or she cannot give legal advice. This is to be determined by a lawyer.

Communication skills

The job of a paralegal requires excellent communication skills in all facets. He or she must be able to listen well and hear detail. He must be able to pick up on non verbal communication from a client. He must be attuned to what the attorney needs and expects. He must be able to read documents thoroughly, and have a good understanding of at least the English language. He must be able to organize data effectively, and present it when it is needed. He must have an understanding of applicable computer programs that will assist in organization and analysis of data. He must understand how to translate this data into well formed and supported arguments or explanations for both clients and attorneys.

Filing system

It is extremely important that a paralegal keeps files well documented and organized. He must develop a system, or adopt one presented by the firm, and be able to locate information quickly as it is needed. Some firms use color coding or number systems to track files. It is best to keep the filing system accessible and centralized so that files can be checked out and returned on a regular basis. Files should be organized in a way that does not allow papers to get lost or moved around, and documents within the file should be kept in chronological order.

Sexual harassment

Each employer should have a sexual harassment policy in place. Sexual harassment is illegal, and includes such unsolicited behaviors as sexual requests whether joking or serious, sexual threats regarding one's position within a company, unwelcome verbal or physical advances, and so forth. Refer to the harassment policy or contact human resources in the event that sexual harassment occurs. No one in an office environment is exempt from following the policies. It is each employee's responsibility to report sexual harassment regardless of whether he or she is the culprit. Any complaint should be addressed without delay. The firm should not only encourage such behavior to be reported, but should also assure that a person who chooses to report harassment will not then be harassed in return.

Recruiting

The purpose of recruiting is to find the applicant best suited for the job. Paralegals may choose to seek employment through a recruitment firm. It is also important for paralegals to network with others in the business, developing a reputation that will help in finding work.

Employers look highly upon paralegals that stay active in associations and stay on the cutting edge of the profession. An employer must be fair in the interview process, judging a potential employee on experience and knowledge, rather than asking about information such as age, religion, and medical condition. The employer may verify that an applicant is legally allowed to work in the United States, but may not question citizenship beyond that.

Fair Labor Standards Act

This act determines how employees are paid for the hours they work, and the maximum number of hours that may be. In most cases, paralegals are non-exempt, which means they must be paid for overtime, and are normally not salaried employees. Generally speaking, an employee who is exempt must be in a managerial position where he or she makes most decision independently, and holds a position that requires an advanced education. Because paralegals are not required or allowed to make many decisions independently regarding their field of work, or law, they are considered specialists rather than professionals, making them non-exempt. Though paralegals are directly supervised by attorneys, many feel that they are independent thinkers, and do very demanding work. Some feel they should be exempt.

General considerations

A paralegal will do best at the job by taking a comprehensive approach. He must understand the attorney's preferences, as well as the daily operations of the law office. He should be familiar with the attorney's long term goals for the practice, and how he can help take part in reaching those goals. For each case, he must understand the clients' needs, and what the individual goals are for that case. He must include himself in developing strategies for how to meet these goals, large and small, so that he can help maintain a proper timeline. The paralegal is vital to the organization of the law firm and each case, and he should be sure that he juggles all that is necessary to meet deadlines and honor the firm's mission.

Basic responsibilities

A paralegal has a general understanding of many of the goings on of a law firm, and can therefore help keep everyone on track. This can be done through effective use of a calendar that includes deadlines for everyone. A paralegal should be sure that clients are billed consistently and correctly. A paralegal will be able to see problems in the way the office is run, and make suggestions as to how things may be improved. For example, a paralegal may be acutely aware that another computer is needed in order to keep accounting records up to date. A paralegal may be aware of a client who needs more frequent communication with the firm, or may see an employee who needs more training and understanding of how the firm operates. A paralegal should be aware of all resources to help with these things, especially if corporate clients can provide assistance in their own areas of expertise.

Obtaining materials

The paralegal should have a general knowledge of the firm, each case, and the ways in which technology can help. A paralegal should be able to assess a case, and determine that perhaps a particular type of database will be needed. The paralegal should then research the cost of the database, train himself on it, and be available to train others as well. The paralegal may need to conduct vendor interviews and obtain bids in order to find the most cost effective purchases. Many of these purchases will be made in bulk, and the paralegal may negotiate for materials the firm may use on a regular basis for presenting evidence in cases, etc. For this, it is good for the paralegal to have a general understanding not only of the firm's long term goals, but also what the firm routinely accomplishes, and what kind of budget it runs off of. A paralegal should never shy away from negotiating on the price of technology and materials from vendors. He should be honest in the negotiations, and know the boundaries of his position.

Managing outside vendors

The paralegal may manage the bidding process for obtaining outside help, be it work, mass document production, or other services. The paralegal should provide enough information for the client, so that the client is aware that the best possible price for services has been negotiated. Often times the client will be billed directly, though some firms maintain an account to cover such purchases. The paralegal should always check to be sure that such services cannot be provided by the client, or obtained by the client at a lower price before settling on the service provider and signing a contract. The paralegal is also responsible for managing the work provided and ensuring that it is correct and of the expected quality. There should be constant open communication about any goods or services being purchased, so that the client is aware of them, and approves them before his or her money is spent.

Maintaining legal resources

In most cases, it is the responsibility of the paralegal to be sure that forms and information specific to the type of law practiced by the firm are obtained and kept well organized for routine reference in a library. The paralegal must be sure that forms are kept in a way that maintains client confidentiality, and that information is changed on them for each client. It is important that resources be kept up to date to ensure that the firm is on the cutting edge of technology and legal information. Much of this information can now be purchased on CD-ROMs including legal databases, or may be researched on the computer. A paralegal must be familiar with how to use these sources.

Library science

If a librarian is not employed to maintain the legal library, it is usually the paralegal's responsibility. He must therefore have a general knowledge of the Dewey Decimal system and the Library of Congress system. He must also develop a way to keep check outs and returns organized, get books back on the shelves in an orderly and timely manner, and keep reference cards organized so books can be found when needed. A paralegal in charge of the library system must not only keep it organized, but also up to date. New information must be obtained at negotiated rates, including proper technology to access information. This includes forms, and periodicals, which may be updated regularly.

Banking account types

Most firms will have an escrow account and a general account for the office. The escrow account is maintained with funds from clients, or funds needed to complete client transactions, such as settlements. The general account for the office is used to maintain payroll and other common office expenses. These two accounts should always be kept separate, regardless of needs. This matter is serious enough that an attorney may be disbarred if the accounts are crossed under his authority. It is therefore extremely important that all spending is documented. A paralegal is responsible for keeping all of his receipts, and providing formal reimbursement requests. A paralegal is also responsible for answering questions about the billing statements provided for clients explaining the details of their account. Though a paralegal may not know in full detail why a client is billed a particular way, or how the attorney manages money for a firm, a general knowledge of the uses and workings of each account is necessary.

Pre-paid legal fees

Many attorneys work off of retainers from corporate clients, or long term cases such as complicated divorces. This means the client pays the attorney an agreed upon rate each month, for ongoing legal advice. The client then knows the attorney is available for advice on an as needed basis, and the attorney can depend on that constant monthly income. Some corporations pre-pay legal fees so that legal advice is available for their customers or employees when necessary. This type of arrangement does not require hourly time tracking, as the fee is unchanging.

Billing ethics

It is extremely important that attorneys and all those working on cases track hours spent working on each case, and what they were doing at the time. This is important for providing accurate reports to the clients of what is being done to further their case, and also so that the client understands exactly what he or she is being billed for. It is a good idea to have a database to track time entries consistently. An arrangement should be made at the beginning of a relationship with a client to determine the frequency of billing, and the way amounts will be determined. The client and paralegal should have a conversation about where outside services will be contracted so that if the client is able to obtain them at a lower rate, it can be arranged. Most importantly, time should be billed as accurately as possible, to protect both the client and the attorney.

Ethical responsibilities

Paralegals must honor confidentiality with clients. They must follow the code of ethics set forth by professional associations they participate in. They must be upfront about the fact that they are paralegals and not lawyers at all times, which means they are not allowed to give legal advice. As long as the paralegal is being supervised by a lawyer and his work is approved, he may perform tasks such as client interviews, research, and drafting articles specific to a case. The paralegal is responsible for doing all of this while maintaining an honest work ethic. All work completed by the paralegal is property of the attorney. The attorney is also directly responsible to the client, therefore it is in his best interest to oversee and manage the working of the paralegal on a regular basis.

Managing workflow

Paralegals will have demands from attorneys and clients, and often work on multiple cases at once. It is important that a paralegal keeps a structured calendar so that he or she is able to estimate how long it will take to complete a task. If a client makes a request, the paralegal should assess the most efficient way to satisfy that request, and delegate it out, or complete it himself. Either way, he should give an estimate to the client of how long to expect the turnaround to be. The same goes for dealings with attorneys. If a paralegal is working on multiple cases, it is his or her responsibility to take on a realistic amount of work, and to be upfront with attorneys about how long it might take to accomplish a task, or if it cannot be done at all, and why. It is the paralegal's responsibilities to be upfront about this, and to honor not only his or own calendar, but also the time frame that others are working on.

Negotiating for assistance

In some cases, there will be too much work for one person to complete by the necessary deadline. In this instance, the paralegal may be in a position to hire outside help, or to call upon other employees in the firm to temporarily stop work for one client in the interest of another. The paralegal must have a clear understanding of how other employees are classified with regard to pay in case there is overtime. In negotiating for extra assistance, the paralegal must have a detailed plan for how to accomplish the goal at hand, and how to utilize the help he or she is requesting. The paralegal must be able to explain why it is necessary, as it will likely cost extra money. If the paralegal is able to show realistic plans for completing the task, as well as proof that he or she is not at fault for the bind, the negotiation will likely result in obtaining some assistance.

Conflicts of interest

A paralegal may have a conflict of interest if he or she has a personal relationship with a client or has worked with many different attorneys who may represent opposing sides of a case. A paralegal needs to be acutely aware of possible conflicts of interest so that he can bring them to the attention of an attorney. It is not acceptable to find a conflict of interest and ignore it. If a paralegal is related to or friends with someone involved with the opposing party, or has a business relationship with someone involved in the case, he or she must be forthright with such information before working on the case. It is also the paralegal's responsibility to watch for conflicts of interest for the attorney.

Trading stocks

A paralegal must always follow protocol when buying and selling public stocks for a client. There must be no conflict of interest here. The paralegal should not trade stocks for a client if he or she has inside knowledge about the company through an outside relationship. The paralegal must also keep any insider information that he has to himself. The paralegal needs to investigate what companies the attorney may have access to non-public information about, and regard those as a conflict of interest as well. The attorney should have a written policy for reference of his exact regulations regarding trading, and they should be strictly followed at all times.

Ethical walls

An ethical wall is a hypothetical wall to protect the person with a conflict of interest from involvement in a case. This person may not speak to the attorneys or other paralegals working on the case as a protection for the client's right to confidentiality. This also protects the paralegal. If an ethical wall is not established and a conflict of interest is not brought to light, the entire legal team can be penalized. It is much more beneficial for the paralegal to recognize the conflict of interest, and move on to a different case. It is then up to the firm to honor the ethical wall by informing all employees of the conflict of interest, and avoiding sharing any information about the case in front of the person with whom there is a conflict.

"Conflicts check"

It is the responsibility of the paralegal to keep a running list of all of the cases and clients he or she has worked with from one firm or attorney to the next. Each time there is a new case, a conflicts check should be performed. In addition, each time new people are added to a case, new witnesses are brought in or new attorneys are added to the legal team, the paralegal must recheck for conflicts. If the paralegal is joining a new firm, a conflicts check must be run regarding all of the cases and clients current with that firm. Many firms will provide a list for reference. It is also important that if a paralegal suspects a conflict of interest, he only shares enough information with the attorney to establish why that conflict exists, minding that he still has an ethical responsibility to honor that client's confidences.

Moral conflicts

If the paralegal feels strongly against the principal of a case he or she is asked to work on, it is important that this is brought to the attention of the supervising attorney. There are no rules that state whether a paralegal is required to work on a case despite his or her personal moral beliefs. Some attorneys will feel that the paralegal should put those beliefs aside just as they do, and work on the case regardless, while others will understand that a strong conflict of morals can lead to below average work. If the paralegal feels that he can put aside his personal beliefs in order to serve the client to the best of his ability, he must also be careful not to let opinions of friends sway his judgment. Attorneys must accept that all clients deserve a fair trial, and a paralegal must determine before working on a case whether or not his morals will get in the way of this.

Confidentiality

It is the paralegal's responsibility to keep all confidential information about a client and a case to himself before, during, and following a case. It is the attorney's responsibility to be sure the paralegal understand which information is confidential, and the importance of keeping it so. It is necessary for the client to share all information with the attorney so that he or she can be represented fairly, and so that the attorney is properly prepared for trial. It is important for the client to trust the attorney; otherwise he may not share all necessary information. The paralegal has the same responsibility as the attorney to honor this confidence, and allow the client to feel at ease. The best rule is that all information regarding any case is confidential. It should never be discussed outside of the case with anyone. Any inside business information or trade secrets of a firm are also confidential.

Attorney-client privilege

The privilege of deciding whether or not to share information in a case as part of an argument is that of the client. It is only with consent of the client, that an attorney can disclose this privileged information. The attorney-client privilege also applies to paralegals, as they are working to represent the attorney. It is the paralegal's responsibility to determine what information may become written record following meetings with a client, etc., as the attorney may prefer that privileged information not be written down where someone else may access it. Likewise, the professional's privy to privileged information should not discuss it where others may hear it. If the privileged information must be written record, it should be marked as such so that the court may honor the status in the case it is requested by subpoena.

Computers and confidentiality

All computers holding confidential information should be password protected, and when the information is no longer needed, it should be removed from the computer altogether. Extra care should be taken with laptops so that information is protected if they get into the wrong hands. If confidential information must be shared over email, the client and paralegal must be sure that no one can view the computer screen, and that no one else has access to the email accounts. Otherwise, privileged information is bound to be shared with persons outside of the case. It is the responsibility of the paralegal and attorney to be sure email is protected before transmitting confidential information. There should always be a disclaimer added to emails in an effort to protect the information if it goes to the wrong person. Notify the reader that information may be accessed by others on the computer, and that the information should not be read by anyone other than the intended recipient.

Unauthorized practices of law

A paralegal must always be upfront with clients, attorneys and other paralegals, that he is not a lawyer. He cannot give legal advice, and he does not directly represent the client. He works for an attorney, and under the attorney's regulation. The attorney is also responsible for understanding the boundaries of a paralegal, and is not to assign any work that may overstep those boundaries. It is the paralegal's responsibility to understand these boundaries, and apply them. For instance, a paralegal will be in the position to act as a liaison between the attorney and client on a regular basis. This will often mean that the paralegal is sharing legal advice from the attorney. The paralegal should always preface the advice by establishing that it comes from the attorney, and should never develop legal advice in addition to that on his own. This applies to cyber communications as well.

Deadlines

The paralegal is responsible for juggling many tasks, and for keeping a well organized calendar in order to manage them properly. Whether the calendar is kept by hand or on a computer, it is the paralegal's most important asset in keeping up with workload, and honoring the ethical responsibilities he has to his supervising attorneys and the clients they represent. The paralegal is responsible for being upfront with an attorney if he cannot complete a requested task in the time frame allotted so that that attorney can find another person to complete the work. If an assignment is confusing, it should be cleared up promptly so that the work is not slowed as a result.

Communicating with other parties

The paralegal must always communicate with another party's representation rather than contacting the client directly. He should only initiate this contact under the direction of his supervising attorney. If dealing with an unrepresented party, it is the paralegal's responsibility to make them aware that the firm cannot advise them. The paralegal must also maintain a professional relationship with the court. He must not speak with jurors or judges in an effort to sway their opinion or to gain advantage for only one side of the case.

Volunteer work

An attorney should encourage employed paralegals to stay up to date with his profession through continuing education opportunities, and volunteer work. The paralegal has an ethical responsibility to use his expertise for the benefit of the community as a volunteer on a regular basis. A paralegal is in a position to help facilitate a more effective legal system for the public, and should use his position to make an effort for such advances. In connection with a supervising attorney, a paralegal should make an effort to help those in need of legal assistance who do not have the means to get it otherwise. A paralegal may stay current in his profession through continuing education and by participating in trade specific associations. Both efforts are an important aspect of being a paralegal, and honoring the profession.

Office Administration terms

Civil Rights Acts of 1964 and 1991: An employer cannot discriminate based on race, color, sex, or nationality. There are high fines for employers who discriminate in these ways.

The Americans with Disabilities Act: An employer must not discriminate against an employee with a disability, and furthermore must willfully address the employee's disability so that he is able to do his job.

The Family Medical Leave Act: This applies to employers with more than 50 employees only. An employee must complete 1,250 hours within a year in order to take advantage of the 12 weeks of unpaid leave offered by an employer. An employee may apply for FMLA based on a pregnancy or adoption, deathly ill family member, or illness of the employee himself. Upon return, the employee is promised the same position, or one of equal status and pay.

The Age Discrimination in Employment Act: This protects employees over 40 years of age from discrimination based on age.

Older Workers Benefit Protection Act: This prohibits an employer from discriminating with allocation of employee benefits based on age, regardless of the additional expense.

The Equal Pay Act: This states that an employer may not discriminate by paying employees differently based on sex. Men and women in the same position are entitled to the same pay.

Contingency fee: This payment is awarded to the attorney only if the client is awarded money. Though it can be a risk for the attorney, the reward is normally at least 33% of the client's settlement.

Percentage fee: The attorney's fee is calculated based on a percentage of what the client receives.

Fixed fee: This type of billing is common in matters that do not involve a client receiving a settlement of money. A fixed fee is applied to legal services such as creating wills or corporations.

Hourly rate: This is common in corporate litigation, and the rate is billable based on who is completing the work. Usually, an attorney charges a different rate for an hour of his work, than for an hour of work by a paralegal. He may also choose to average the rates of employees assigned to the case, and bill one constant rate.

Technology in the Law

Computerized databases

A computerized database can be used to quickly and accurately obtain and sort information. One way databases are used in many law firms is to help determine conflicts of interest. A paralegal can run a report in the database requesting all information related to the client, and immediately reveal possible conflicts of interest if the database is manipulated correctly. Databases are also very helpful in creating calendars and to-do lists so that deadlines are met, and responsible parties for each part of a job are clear. Industry specific databases can be purchased to help in tracking deadlines, appointments, reminders, etc.

Storing documents

A database can be used in place of physical stacks of papers to allow for fast retrieval of documents, and more efficient storage. Documents can be scanned and saved to disks. This can be done either by using a scanner that creates a digital image of the document as it is, or by using software called OCR which actually interprets the words in the documents so that key word searches can be performed. OCR is not a perfect science, and in order to use it to its full advantage, each document needs to be edited once it is scanned. If image software is used, then a relational database must be created in order to store and retrieve the documents and information within them. Maintaining a database is a cost effective and efficient way to house information and retrieve it when necessary.

Deposition summarization software

Full transcripts of court proceedings are taken down by court reporters and saved to disks for reference. A law firm may choose to purchase software that can organize and retrieve information in the depositions for future use. This allows a firm to manipulate the transcripts and highlight information helpful to their case. The information can be organized in a number of ways, depending on the goal of the user. Software is also available that will translate documents that are created using shorthand into plain English. This software is used by the court reporter to provide a readable rough draft of the proceedings immediately.

Case management and the internet

The most commonly used feature of the internet within law firms is email. Email can be used to discuss cases, review drafted contracts, and express deadlines with busy attorneys on a daily basis. It is a convenient way to communicate, and printing an email provides a written record of correspondence. Intranets and extranets can be set up to allow specific people access to information from the convenience of their own computers. Common documents can be housed there such as calendars and other databases that many people may need to access. The internet is also a great research tool, connecting many different resources that may be useful in a case.

Computer assisted legal research

Legal research through the use of a computer has become the most widely used form of legal research used today. There are two prominent legal research databases, Westlaw and Lexis, which house information paralegals may need in case research. A researcher can use these databases much like internal ones housed by the firm, or like the internet. They allow key word searches to guide a user to relevant information. Both databases also allow the user to search using plain English so that information can be retrieved regarding subjects of which the user has little knowledge. Both databases are regularly updated with new court decisions and information so that the user is getting relevant information.

Word processing

Most every law firm will apply word processing using major word processing software. Word processing is done on a computer and allows the documents to be created, stored, accessed, and re-used when needed. When used to its full advantage, word processing can save a user from retyping phrases that are commonly used, by applying key commands to bring them up and insert them into a working document. Forms can also be created to save time with commonly created documents such as letters and contracts.

Software

It is important that a paralegal is able to assess the needs of a law office and make suggestions regarding new software that might help manage work more effectively. Some offices hire technology consultants to take on this responsibility, purchase the software, and train the employees. It is important that however software is acquired; employees are trained to use it effectively. This will help avoid costly mistakes, and take full advantage of what the software has to offer. If a paralegal sees a need for specific software, he must prepare a request for proposal that dictates exactly what the firm needs, and for what purpose. Vendors will be able to assist the firm most effectively if a good request for proposal is submitted.

Time keeping and billing

Particularly if a client is to be billed on an hourly rate, tracking work on a computer is advantageous when creating an accurate bill. Software designed for billing and tracking accounts can allow the user to analyze statements and run reports for specific clients, specific employees, or run cost analyses on a case. Software can help track time worked for a specific client, and even what the work consists of. From this invoices and statements can be created. Sophisticated software can help manage all accounts held by the law firm, and track amount of work and time spent on specific projects by employees.

Important terms

Scanning: Refers to the digital capture of an image to be saved on a computer or disk.

Dpi: Describes the resolution of a scanned image based on the number of dots per inch. A higher number of dots per inch refers to a better quality resolution of the image.

Coding: Taking important components of a document and entering them into a database.

CD-ROM: A compact disk that contains read only memory to be retrieved when needed.

Jukebox: A large case to hold multiple CDs.

Secret Key #1 - Time is Your Greatest Enemy

Pace Yourself

Wear a watch. At the beginning of the test, check the time (or start a chronometer on your watch to count the minutes), and check the time after every few questions to make sure you are "on schedule."

If you are forced to speed up, do it efficiently. Usually one or more answer choices can be eliminated without too much difficulty. Above all, don't panic. Don't speed up and just begin guessing at random choices. By pacing yourself, and continually monitoring your progress against your watch, you will always know exactly how far ahead or behind you are with your available time. If you find that you are one minute behind on the test, don't skip one question without spending any time on it, just to catch back up. Take 15 fewer seconds on the next four questions, and after four questions you'll have caught back up. Once you catch back up, you can continue working each problem at your normal pace.

Furthermore, don't dwell on the problems that you were rushed on. If a problem was taking up too much time and you made a hurried guess, it must be difficult. The difficult questions are the ones you are most likely to miss anyway, so it isn't a big loss. It is better to end with more time than you need than to run out of time.

Lastly, sometimes it is beneficial to slow down if you are constantly getting ahead of time. You are always more likely to catch a careless mistake by working more slowly than quickly, and among very high-scoring test takers (those who are likely to have lots of time left over), careless errors affect the score more than mastery of material.

Secret Key #2 - Guessing is not Guesswork

You probably know that guessing is a good idea - unlike other standardized tests, there is no penalty for getting a wrong answer. Even if you have no idea about a question, you still have a 20-25% chance of getting it right.

Most test takers do not understand the impact that proper guessing can have on their score. Unless you score extremely high, guessing will significantly contribute to your final score.

Monkeys Take the Test

What most test takers don't realize is that to insure that 20-25% chance, you have to guess randomly. If you put 20 monkeys in a room to take this test, assuming they answered once per question and behaved themselves, on average they would get 20-25% of the questions correct. Put 20 test takers in the room, and the average will be much lower among guessed questions. Why?

1. The test writers intentionally writes deceptive answer choices that "look" right. A test taker has no idea about a question, so picks the "best looking" answer, which is often wrong. The monkey has no idea what looks good and what doesn't, so will consistently be lucky about 20-25% of the time.

2. Test takers will eliminate answer choices from the guessing pool based on a hunch or intuition. Simple but correct answers often get excluded, leaving a 0% chance of being correct. The monkey has no clue, and often gets lucky with the best choice.

This is why the process of elimination endorsed by most test courses is flawed and detrimental to your performance- test takers don't guess, they make an ignorant stab in the dark that is usually worse than random.

$5 Challenge

Let me introduce one of the most valuable ideas of this course- the $5 challenge:

You only mark your "best guess" if you are willing to bet $5 on it.
You only eliminate choices from guessing if you are willing to bet $5 on it.

Why $5? Five dollars is an amount of money that is small yet not insignificant, and can really add up fast (20 questions could cost you $100). Likewise, each answer choice on one question of the test will have a small impact on your overall score, but it can really add up to a lot of points in the end.

The process of elimination IS valuable. The following shows your chance of guessing it right:

If you eliminate wrong answer choices until only this many remain:	1	2	3
Chance of getting it correct:	100%	50%	33%

However, if you accidentally eliminate the right answer or go on a hunch for an incorrect answer, your chances drop dramatically: to 0%. By guessing among all the answer choices, you are GUARANTEED to have a shot at the right answer.

That's why the $5 test is so valuable- if you give up the advantage and safety of a pure guess, it had better be worth the risk.

What we still haven't covered is how to be sure that whatever guess you make is truly random. Here's the easiest way:

Always pick the first answer choice among those remaining.

Such a technique means that you have decided, **before you see a single test question**, exactly how you are going to guess- and since the order of choices tells you nothing about which one is correct, this guessing technique is perfectly random.

This section is not meant to scare you away from making educated guesses or eliminating choices- you just need to define when a choice is worth eliminating. The $5 test, along with a pre-defined random guessing strategy, is the best way to make sure you reap all of the benefits of guessing.

Secret Key #3 - Practice Smarter, Not Harder

Many test takers delay the test preparation process because they dread the awful amounts of practice time they think necessary to succeed on the test. We have refined an effective method that will take you only a fraction of the time.

There are a number of "obstacles" in your way to succeed. Among these are answering questions, finishing in time, and mastering test-taking strategies. All must be executed on the day of the test at peak performance, or your score will suffer. The test is a mental marathon that has a large impact on your future.

Just like a marathon runner, it is important to work your way up to the full challenge. So first you just worry about questions, and then time, and finally strategy:

Success Strategy

1. Find a good source for practice tests.
2. If you are willing to make a larger time investment, consider using more than one study guide- often the different approaches of multiple authors will help you "get" difficult concepts.
3. Take a practice test with no time constraints, with all study helps "open book." Take your time with questions and focus on applying strategies.
4. Take a practice test with time constraints, with all guides "open book."
5. Take a final practice test with no open material and time limits

If you have time to take more practice tests, just repeat step 5. By gradually exposing yourself to the full rigors of the test environment, you will condition your mind to the stress of test day and maximize your success.

Secret Key #4 - Prepare, Don't Procrastinate

Let me state an obvious fact: if you take the test three times, you will get three different scores. This is due to the way you feel on test day, the level of preparedness you have, and, despite the test writers' claims to the contrary, some tests WILL be easier for you than others.

Since your future depends so much on your score, you should maximize your chances of success. In order to maximize the likelihood of success, you've got to prepare in advance. This means taking practice tests and spending time learning the information and test taking strategies you will need to succeed.

Never take the test as a "practice" test, expecting that you can just take it again if you need to. Feel free to take sample tests on your own, but when you go to take the official test, be prepared, be focused, and do your best the first time!

Secret Key #5 - Test Yourself

Everyone knows that time is money. There is no need to spend too much of your time or too little of your time preparing for the test. You should only spend as much of your precious time preparing as is necessary for you to get the score you need.

Once you have taken a practice test under real conditions of time constraints, then you will know if you are ready for the test or not.

If you have scored extremely high the first time that you take the practice test, then there is not much point in spending countless hours studying. You are already there.

Benchmark your abilities by retaking practice tests and seeing how much you have improved. Once you score high enough to guarantee success, then you are ready.

If you have scored well below where you need, then knuckle down and begin studying in earnest. Check your improvement regularly through the use of practice tests under real conditions. Above all, don't worry, panic, or give up. The key is perseverance!

Then, when you go to take the test, remain confident and remember how well you did on the practice tests. If you can score high enough on a practice test, then you can do the same on the real thing.

General Strategies

The most important thing you can do is to ignore your fears and jump into the test immediately- do not be overwhelmed by any strange-sounding terms. You have to jump into the test like jumping into a pool- all at once is the easiest way.

Make Predictions

As you read and understand the question, try to guess what the answer will be. Remember that several of the answer choices are wrong, and once you begin reading them, your mind will immediately become cluttered with answer choices designed to throw you off. Your mind is typically the most focused immediately after you have read the question and digested its contents. If you can, try to predict what the correct answer will be. You may be surprised at what you can predict.

Quickly scan the choices and see if your prediction is in the listed answer choices. If it is, then you can be quite confident that you have the right answer. It still won't hurt to check the other answer choices, but most of the time, you've got it!

Answer the Question

It may seem obvious to only pick answer choices that answer the question, but the test writers can create some excellent answer choices that are wrong. Don't pick an answer just because it sounds right, or you believe it to be true. It MUST answer the question. Once you've made your selection, always go back and check it against the question and make sure that you didn't misread the question, and the answer choice does answer the question posed.

Benchmark

After you read the first answer choice, decide if you think it sounds correct or not. If it doesn't, move on to the next answer choice. If it does, mentally mark that answer choice. This doesn't mean that you've definitely selected it as your answer choice, it just means that it's the best you've seen thus far. Go ahead and read the next choice. If the next choice is worse than the one you've already selected, keep going to the next answer choice. If the next choice is better than the choice you've already selected, mentally mark the new answer choice as your best guess.

The first answer choice that you select becomes your standard. Every other answer choice must be benchmarked against that standard. That choice is correct until proven otherwise by another answer choice beating it out. Once you've decided that no other answer choice seems as good, do one final check to ensure that your answer choice answers the question posed.

Valid Information

Don't discount any of the information provided in the question. Every piece of information may be necessary to determine the correct answer. None of the information in the question is there to throw you off (while the answer choices will certainly have information to throw you off). If two seemingly unrelated topics are discussed, don't ignore either. You can be confident there is a relationship, or it wouldn't be included in the question, and you are probably going to have to determine what is that relationship to find the answer.

Avoid "Fact Traps"

Don't get distracted by a choice that is factually true. Your search is for the answer that answers the question. Stay focused and don't fall for an answer that is true but incorrect. Always go back to the question and make sure you're choosing an answer that actually answers the question and is not just a true statement. An answer can be factually correct, but it MUST answer the question asked. Additionally, two answers can both be seemingly correct, so be sure to read all of the answer choices, and make sure that you get the one that BEST answers the question.

Milk the Question

Some of the questions may throw you completely off. They might deal with a subject you have not been exposed to, or one that you haven't reviewed in years. While your lack of knowledge about the subject will be a hindrance, the question itself can give you many clues that will help you find the correct answer. Read the question carefully and look for clues. Watch particularly for adjectives and nouns describing difficult terms or words that you don't recognize. Regardless of if you completely understand a word or not, replacing it with a synonym either provided or one you more familiar with may help you to understand what the questions are asking. Rather than wracking your mind about specific detailed information concerning a difficult term or word, try to use mental substitutes that are easier to understand.

The Trap of Familiarity

Don't just choose a word because you recognize it. On difficult questions, you may not recognize a number of words in the answer choices. The test writers don't put "make-believe" words on the test; so don't think that just because you only recognize all the words in one answer choice means that answer choice must be correct. If you only recognize words in one answer choice, then focus on that one. Is it correct? Try your best to determine if it is correct. If it is, that is great, but if it doesn't, eliminate it. Each word and answer choice you eliminate increases your chances of getting the question correct, even if you then have to guess among the unfamiliar choices.

Eliminate Answers

Eliminate choices as soon as you realize they are wrong. But be careful! Make sure you consider all of the possible answer choices. Just because one appears right, doesn't mean that the next one won't be even better! The test writers will usually put more than one good answer choice for every question, so read all of them. Don't worry if you are stuck between two that seem right. By getting down to just two remaining possible choices, your odds are now 50/50. Rather than wasting too much time, play the odds. You are guessing, but guessing wisely, because you've been able to knock out some of the answer choices that you know are wrong. If you are eliminating choices and realize that the last answer choice you are left with is also obviously wrong, don't panic. Start over and consider each choice again. There may easily be something that you missed the first time and will realize on the second pass.

Tough Questions

If you are stumped on a problem or it appears too hard or too difficult, don't waste time. Move on! Remember though, if you can quickly check for obviously incorrect answer choices, your chances of guessing correctly are greatly improved. Before you completely give up, at least try to knock out a couple of possible answers. Eliminate what you can and then guess at the remaining answer choices before moving on.

Brainstorm

If you get stuck on a difficult question, spend a few seconds quickly brainstorming. Run through the complete list of possible answer choices. Look at each choice and ask yourself, "Could this answer the question satisfactorily?" Go through each answer choice and consider it independently of the other. By systematically going through all possibilities, you may find something that you would otherwise overlook. Remember that when you get stuck, it's important to try to keep moving.

Read Carefully

Understand the problem. Read the question and answer choices carefully. Don't miss the question because you misread the terms. You have plenty of time to read each question thoroughly and make sure you understand what is being asked. Yet a happy medium must be attained, so don't waste too much time. You must read carefully, but efficiently.

Face Value

When in doubt, use common sense. Always accept the situation in the problem at face value. Don't read too much into it. These problems will not require you to make huge leaps of logic. The test writers aren't trying to throw you off with a cheap trick. If you have to go beyond creativity and make a leap of logic in order to have an answer choice answer the question, then you should look at the other answer choices. Don't overcomplicate the problem by creating theoretical relationships or explanations that will warp time or space. These are normal problems rooted in reality. It's just that the applicable relationship or explanation may not be readily apparent and you have to figure things out. Use your common sense to interpret anything that isn't clear.

Prefixes

If you're having trouble with a word in the question or answer choices, try dissecting it. Take advantage of every clue that the word might include. Prefixes and suffixes can be a huge help. Usually they allow you to determine a basic meaning. Pre- means before, post- means after, pro - is positive, de- is negative. From these prefixes and suffixes, you can get an idea of the general meaning of the word and try to put it into context. Beware though of any traps. Just because con is the opposite of pro, doesn't necessarily mean congress is the opposite of progress!

Hedge Phrases

Watch out for critical "hedge" phrases, such as likely, may, can, will often, sometimes, often, almost, mostly, usually, generally, rarely, sometimes. Question writers insert these hedge phrases to cover every possibility. Often an answer choice will be wrong simply because it leaves no room for exception. Avoid answer choices that have definitive words like "exactly," and "always".

Switchback Words

Stay alert for "switchbacks". These are the words and phrases frequently used to alert you to shifts in thought. The most common switchback word is "but". Others include although, however, nevertheless, on the other hand, even though, while, in spite of, despite, regardless of.

New Information

Correct answer choices will rarely have completely new information included. Answer choices typically are straightforward reflections of the material asked about and will directly relate to the question. If a new piece of information is included in an answer choice that doesn't even seem to relate to the topic being asked about, then that answer choice is likely incorrect. All of the information needed to answer the question is usually provided for you, and so you should not have to make guesses that are unsupported or choose answer choices that require unknown information that cannot be reasoned on its own.

Time Management

On technical questions, don't get lost on the technical terms. Don't spend too much time on any one question. If you don't know what a term means, then since you don't have a dictionary, odds are you aren't going to get much further. You should immediately recognize terms as whether or not you know them. If you don't, work with the other clues that you have, the other answer choices and terms provided, but don't waste too much time trying to figure out a difficult term.

Contextual Clues

Look for contextual clues. An answer can be right but not correct. The contextual clues will help you find the answer that is most right and is correct. Understand the context in which a phrase or statement is made. This will help you make important distinctions.

Don't Panic

Panicking will not answer any questions for you. Therefore, it isn't helpful. When you first see the question, if your mind goes blank, take a deep breath. Force yourself to mechanically go through the steps of solving the problem and using the strategies you've learned.

Pace Yourself

Don't get clock fever. It's easy to be overwhelmed when you're looking at a page full of questions, your mind is full of random thoughts and feeling confused, and the clock is ticking down faster than you would like. Calm down and maintain the pace that you have set for yourself. As long as you are on track by monitoring your pace, you are guaranteed to have enough time for yourself. When you get to the last few minutes of the test, it may seem like you won't have enough time left, but if you only have as many questions as you should have left at that point, then you're right on track!

Answer Selection

The best way to pick an answer choice is to eliminate all of those that are wrong, until only one is left and confirm that is the correct answer. Sometimes though, an answer choice may immediately look right. Be careful! Take a second to make sure that the other choices are not equally obvious. Don't make a hasty mistake. There are only two times that you should stop before checking other answers. First is when you are positive that the answer choice you have selected is correct. Second is when time is almost out and you have to make a quick guess!

Check Your Work

Since you will probably not know every term listed and the answer to every question, it is important that you get credit for the ones that you do know. Don't miss any questions through careless mistakes. If at all possible, try to take a second to look back over your answer selection and make sure you've selected the correct answer choice and haven't made a costly careless mistake (such as marking an answer choice that you didn't mean to mark). This quick double check should more than pay for itself in caught mistakes for the time it costs.

Beware of Directly Quoted Answers

Sometimes an answer choice will repeat word for word a portion of the question or reference section. However, beware of such exact duplication – it may be a trap! More than likely, the correct choice will paraphrase or summarize a point, rather than being exactly the same wording.

Slang

Scientific sounding answers are better than slang ones. An answer choice that begins "To compare the outcomes…" is much more likely to be correct than one that begins "Because some people insisted…"

Extreme Statements

Avoid wild answers that throw out highly controversial ideas that are proclaimed as established fact. An answer choice that states the "process should be used in certain situations, if…" is much more likely to be correct than one that states the "process should be discontinued completely."   The first is a calm rational statement and doesn't even make a definitive, uncompromising stance, using a hedge word "if" to provide wiggle room, whereas the second choice is a radical idea and far more extreme.

Answer Choice Families

When you have two or more answer choices that are direct opposites or parallels, one of them is usually the correct answer. For instance, if one answer choice states "x increases" and another answer choice states "x decreases" or "y increases," then those two or three answer choices are very similar in construction and fall into the same family of answer choices. A family of answer choices is when two or three answer choices are very similar in construction, and yet often have a directly opposite meaning.   Usually the correct answer choice will be in that family of answer choices. The "odd man out" or answer choice that doesn't seem to fit the parallel construction of the other answer choices is more likely to be incorrect.

Special Report: What Your Test Score Will Tell You About Your IQ

Did you know that most standardized tests correlate very strongly with IQ? In fact, your general intelligence is a better predictor of your success than any other factor, and most tests intentionally measure this trait to some degree to ensure that those selected by the test are truly qualified for the test's purposes.

Before we can delve into the relation between your test score and IQ, I will first have to explain what exactly is IQ. Here's the formula:

Your IQ = 100 + (Number of standard deviations below or above the average)*15

Now, let's define standard deviations by using an example. If we have 5 people with 5 different heights, then first we calculate the average. Let's say the average was 65 inches. The standard deviation is the "average distance" away from the average of each of the members. It is a direct measure of variability - if the 5 people included Jackie Chan and Shaquille O'Neal, obviously there's a lot more variability in that group than a group of 5 sisters who are all within 6 inches in height of each other. The standard deviation uses a number to characterize the average range of difference within a group.

A convenient feature of most groups is that they have a "normal" distribution- makes sense that most things would be normal, right? Without getting into a bunch of statistical mumbo-jumbo, you just need to know that if you know the average of the group and the standard deviation, you can successfully predict someone's percentile rank in the group.

Confused? Let me give you an example. If instead of 5 people's heights, we had 100 people, we could figure out their rank in height JUST by knowing the average, standard deviation, and their height. We wouldn't need to know each person's height and manually rank them, we could just predict their rank based on three numbers.

What this means is that you can take your PERCENTILE rank that is often given with your test and relate this to your RELATIVE IQ of people taking the test - that is, your IQ relative to the people taking the test. Obviously, there's no way to know your actual IQ because the people taking a standardized test are usually not very good samples of the general population- many of those with extremely low IQ's never achieve a level of success or competency necessary to complete a typical standardized test. In fact, professional psychologists who measure IQ actually have to use non-written tests that can fairly measure the IQ of those not able to complete a traditional test.

The bottom line is to not take your test score too seriously, but it is fun to compute your "relative IQ" among the people who took the test with you. I've done the calculations below. Just look up your percentile rank in the left and then you'll see your "relative IQ" for your test in the right hand column-

Percentile Rank	Your Relative IQ		Percentile Rank	Your Relative IQ
99	135		59	103
98	131		58	103
97	128		57	103
96	126		56	102
95	125		55	102
94	123		54	102
93	122		53	101
92	121		52	101
91	120		51	100
90	119		50	100
89	118		49	100
88	118		48	99
87	117		47	99
86	116		46	98
85	116		45	98
84	115		44	98
83	114		43	97
82	114		42	97
81	113		41	97
80	113		40	96
79	112		39	96
78	112		38	95
77	111		37	95
76	111		36	95
75	110		35	94
74	110		34	94
73	109		33	93
72	109		32	93
71	108		31	93
70	108		30	92
69	107		29	92
68	107		28	91
67	107		27	91
66	106		26	90
65	106		25	90
64	105		24	89
63	105		23	89
62	105		22	88
61	104		21	88
60	104		20	87

Special Report: What is Test Anxiety and How to Overcome It?

The very nature of tests caters to some level of anxiety, nervousness or tension, just as we feel for any important event that occurs in our lives. A little bit of anxiety or nervousness can be a good thing. It helps us with motivation, and makes achievement just that much sweeter. However, too much anxiety can be a problem; especially if it hinders our ability to function and perform.

"Test anxiety," is the term that refers to the emotional reactions that some test-takers experience when faced with a test or exam. Having a fear of testing and exams is based upon a rational fear, since the test-taker's performance can shape the course of an academic career. Nevertheless, experiencing excessive fear of examinations will only interfere with the test-takers ability to perform, and his/her chances to be successful.

There are a large variety of causes that can contribute to the development and sensation of test anxiety. These include, but are not limited to lack of performance and worrying about issues surrounding the test.

Lack of Preparation

Lack of preparation can be identified by the following behaviors or situations:

Not scheduling enough time to study, and therefore cramming the night before the test or exam

Managing time poorly, to create the sensation that there is not enough time to do everything

Failing to organize the text information in advance, so that the study material consists of the entire text and not simply the pertinent information

Poor overall studying habits

Worrying, on the other hand, can be related to both the test taker, or many other factors around him/her that will be affected by the results of the test. These include worrying about:

Previous performances on similar exams, or exams in general

How friends and other students are achieving

The negative consequences that will result from a poor grade or failure

There are three primary elements to test anxiety. Physical components, which involve the same typical bodily reactions as those to acute anxiety (to be discussed below). Emotional factors have to do with fear or panic. Mental or cognitive issues concerning attention spans and memory abilities.

Physical Signals

There are many different symptoms of test anxiety, and these are not limited to mental and emotional strain. Frequently there are a range of physical signals that will let a test taker know that he/she is suffering from test anxiety. These bodily changes can include the following:

Perspiring

Sweaty palms

Wet, trembling hands

Nausea

Dry mouth

A knot in the stomach

Headache

Faintness

Muscle tension

Aching shoulders, back and neck

Rapid heart beat

Feeling too hot/cold

To recognize the sensation of test anxiety, a test-taker should monitor him/herself for the following sensations:

The physical distress symptoms as listed above

Emotional sensitivity, expressing emotional feelings such as the need to cry or laugh too much, or a sensation of anger or helplessness

A decreased ability to think, causing the test-taker to blank out or have racing thoughts that are hard to organize or control.

Though most students will feel some level of anxiety when faced with a test or exam, the majority can cope with that anxiety and maintain it at a manageable level. However, those who cannot are faced with a very real and very serious condition, which can and should be controlled for the immeasurable benefit of this sufferer.

Naturally, these sensations lead to negative results for the testing experience. The most common effects of test anxiety have to do with nervousness and mental blocking.

Nervousness

Nervousness can appear in several different levels:

The test-taker's difficulty, or even inability to read and understand the questions on the test

The difficulty or inability to organize thoughts to a coherent form

The difficulty or inability to recall key words and concepts relating to the testing questions (especially essays)

The receipt of poor grades on a test, though the test material was well known by the test taker

Conversely, a person may also experience mental blocking, which involves:

Blanking out on test questions

Only remembering the correct answers to the questions when the test has already finished.

Fortunately for test anxiety sufferers, beating these feelings, to a large degree, has to do with proper preparation. When a test taker has a feeling of preparedness, then anxiety will be dramatically lessened.

The first step to resolving anxiety issues is to distinguish which of the two types of anxiety are being suffered. If the anxiety is a direct result of a lack of preparation, this should be considered a normal reaction, and the anxiety level (as opposed to the test results) shouldn't be anything to worry about. However, if, when adequately prepared, the test-taker still panics, blanks out, or seems to overreact, this is not a fully rational reaction. While this can be considered normal too, there are many ways to combat and overcome these effects.

Remember that anxiety cannot be entirely eliminated, however, there are ways to minimize it, to make the anxiety easier to manage. Preparation is one of the best ways to minimize test anxiety. Therefore the following techniques are wise in order to best fight off any anxiety that may want to build.

To begin with, try to avoid cramming before a test, whenever it is possible. By trying to memorize an entire term's worth of information in one day, you'll be shocking your system, and not giving yourself a very good chance to absorb the information. This is an easy path to anxiety, so for those who suffer from test anxiety, cramming should not even be considered an option.

Instead of cramming, work throughout the semester to combine all of the material which is presented throughout the semester, and work on it gradually as the course goes by, making sure to master the main concepts first, leaving minor details for a week or so before the test.

To study for the upcoming exam, be sure to pose questions that may be on the examination, to gauge the ability to answer them by integrating the ideas from your texts, notes and lectures, as well as any supplementary readings.

If it is truly impossible to cover all of the information that was covered in that particular term, concentrate on the most important portions, that can be covered very well. Learn these concepts as best as possible, so that when the test comes, a goal can be made to use these concepts as presentations of your knowledge.

In addition to study habits, changes in attitude are critical to beating a struggle with test anxiety. In fact, an improvement of the perspective over the entire test-taking experience can actually help a test taker to enjoy studying and therefore improve the overall experience. Be certain not to overemphasize the significance of the grade - know that the result of the test is neither a reflection of self worth, nor is it a measure of intelligence; one grade will not predict a person's future success.

To improve an overall testing outlook, the following steps should be tried:

Keeping in mind that the most reasonable expectation for taking a test is to expect to try to demonstrate as much of what you know as you possibly can. Reminding ourselves that a test is only one test; this is not the only one, and there will be others.
The thought of thinking of oneself in an irrational, all-or-nothing term should be avoided at all costs.
A reward should be designated for after the test, so there's something to look forward to. Whether it be going to a movie, going out to eat, or simply visiting friends, schedule it in advance, and do it no matter what result is expected on the exam.

Test-takers should also keep in mind that the basics are some of the most important things, even beyond anti-anxiety techniques and studying. Never neglect the basic social, emotional and biological needs, in order to try to absorb information. In order to best achieve, these three factors must be held as just as important as the studying itself.

Study Steps

Remember the following important steps for studying:

Maintain healthy nutrition and exercise habits. Continue both your recreational activities and social pass times. These both contribute to your physical and emotional well being.

Be certain to get a good amount of sleep, especially the night before the test, because when you're overtired you are not able to perform to the best of your best ability.

Keep the studying pace to a moderate level by taking breaks when they are needed, and varying the work whenever possible, to keep the mind fresh instead of getting bored.

When enough studying has been done that all the material that can be learned has been learned, and the test taker is prepared for the test, stop studying and do something relaxing such as listening to music, watching a movie, or taking a warm bubble bath.

There are also many other techniques to minimize the uneasiness or apprehension that is experienced along with test anxiety before, during, or even after the examination. In fact, there are a great deal of things that can be done to stop anxiety from interfering with lifestyle and performance. Again, remember that anxiety will not be eliminated entirely, and it shouldn't be. Otherwise that "up" feeling for exams would not exist, and most of us depend on that sensation to perform better than usual. However, this anxiety has to be at a level that is manageable.

Of course, as we have just discussed, being prepared for the exam is half the battle right away. Attending all classes, finding out what knowledge will be expected on the exam, and knowing the exam schedules are easy steps to lowering anxiety. Keeping up with work will remove the need to cram, and efficient study habits will eliminate wasted time. Studying should be done in an ideal location for concentration, so that it is simple to become interested in the material and give it complete attention. A method such as SQ3R (Survey, Question, Read, Recite, Review) is a wonderful key to follow to make sure that the study habits are as effective as possible, especially in the case of learning from a textbook. Flashcards are great techniques for memorization. Learning to